Festive Foods for the Holidays™

A Hanukkah Holiday COOKBOOK

Emily Raabe

The Rosen Publishing Group's
PowerKids Press™
New York

The recipes in this cookbook
are intended for a child to make together with an adult.

Many thanks to Ruth Rosen and her test kitchen

For Rachel, my favorite chef

Published in 2002 by The Rosen Publishing Group, Inc.
29 East 21st Street, New York, NY 10010

First Edition

Book Design: Maria E. Melendez
Project Editor: Frances E. Ruffin

Photo Credits: Cover (family) © Dave Bartruff/CORBIS; cover and title page (oil lamp, menorah candles) © IndexStock; cover and title page (cheeses) © SuperStock; pp. 4, 12 © Richard T. Nowitz/CORBIS; p. 7 © Bettmann/CORBIS; p. 8 (battle) © Archivo Iconografico, S.A./CORBIS; p. 11 © Owen Franken/CORBIS; pp. 15 (yams), 17 (cloves), 19 (cheeses), 21 (brown sugar) © StockFood America; dreidel page number designs illustrated by Maria E. Melendez.

Raabe, Emily.
   A Hanukkah holiday cookbook / Emily Raabe. —1st ed.
        p. cm. — (Festive foods for the holidays)
Includes index.
   ISBN 0–8239–5626–1 (lib. bdg.)
 1. Hanukkah cookery—Juvenile literature. [1. Hanukkah. 2. Hanukkah cookery. 3. Cookery, Jewish. 4. Holidays.] I. Title. II. Series.
   TX739.2.H35 R33 2002
   641.5'676—dc21

                                                                                    00—012305

Manufactured in the United States of America

Contents

What Is Hanukkah?

Every year, Jewish people around the world celebrate a holiday called Hanukkah, or the Festival of Lights. Hanukkah comes during the middle of winter, when the days are short and cold. It is a time of celebration and feasting. Hanukkah celebrates the spirit of the Jewish people by remembering a story about a group of Jews known as the Maccabees. Thousands of years ago, the Maccabees fought to **defend** their religion from the Syrian king. During Hanukkah, Jewish people eat certain foods, tell stories, and sing songs that remind them of the Maccabees and their fight for freedom.

Families all over the world gather together to celebrate Hanukkah each year.

When Is Hanukkah?

Hanukkah has been celebrated for more than 2,000 years. It happens every winter for eight days, beginning on the twenty-fifth day of the Jewish calendar month of Kislev. The Jewish calendar is a special calendar that uses the **cycles** of the moon to tell the time of year. The regular calendar uses the sun. That means Hanukkah may fall on different days every year. It is, however, always celebrated near the end of November or December. The sixth night of Hanukkah comes on a **new moon**.

6

The new moon greets the sixth night of Hanukkah each year.

The Story of the Maccabees

About 2,400 years ago, the Jewish people lived in Judea, the country that we now know as Israel. The king of Syria, which was a country next to Judea, also ruled Judea. This king was named Antiochus. Antiochus wanted the Jews to **worship** his gods. He didn't want them to worship the God of their religion. Their religion was **Judaism**. One family refused to follow the king's orders. This family and their followers became known as the Maccabees. This is because maccabee means hammer in **Hebrew**, and these Jews struck at the Syrian armies like hammers. The Maccabees fought the Syrians for three years. When they won the final battle, they marched home into the city of Jerusalem.

The Maccabees fought many fierce battles to win their freedom.

9

A Festival of Lights

After winning the battle against the Syrians, the Jewish people returned to the temple in Jerusalem that the Syrian soldiers had destroyed. They cleaned the temple and made it holy like it was before. Then they held a special celebration. This celebration was the first Hanukkah. The Jewish people rededicated the temple to God by burning oil in a lamp. They needed to find oil that had not been touched and made dirty by the Syrians. After a careful search of the temple, one good container of oil was found. It was enough for only one day. According to the Bible, God performed a **miracle** and made the oil last for eight days and eight nights. During Hanukkah, Jewish people remember this miracle by lighting candles.

10

Special candles are lit during Hanukkah to remind the Jews of an ancient miracle.

The Hanukkah Menorah

Each night of Hanukkah, at sundown, Jewish people light candles in a special candleholder called a menorah. The menorah holds nine candles, one for each of the eight nights of Hanukkah, plus one that is used to light the other candles. The ninth candle is called the helper because it helps to light the others. It is used to light one candle on the first night. Each night of Hanukkah, another candle in the menorah is lit, until all eight candles are burning brightly. The menorah candles **symbolize** the light of peace that followed the long years of darkness and war between the Jewish people and the Syrians. They also symbolize the light that the Maccabees burned in the temple after the war.

Prayers are said over the menorah in Hebrew, the language spoken by the Maccabees.

13

Eating Latkes

Many Jewish people eat latkes during Hanukkah. Latke is the Hebrew word for pancake. Latkes are thin pancakes, made of potatoes, that have been fried in oil. It's a custom to eat foods fried in oil to remember the miracle of the oil that kept the temple lamp burning for eight nights. Although latkes are a popular food at many people's Hanukkah celebration, the Maccabees themselves never ate latkes because there were no potatoes in Judea where they lived. Potatoes were brought to Europe from South America a long time after the Maccabees lived. Latkes first were made in Eastern Europe in the 1600s.

Potato Latkes

You will need:

3 white potatoes,
  peeled and grated
1 medium-size sweet
  potato, peeled and
  grated
1 medium-size onion,
  grated
2 eggs, slightly beaten
1 teaspoon (5 ml) salt
¼ teaspoon (1.2 ml)
  black pepper

¾ cup (177 ml)
  matzo meal
  (found in ethnic
  section of
  supermarket)
½ cup (119 ml)
  vegetable oil for
  frying.

How to do it:

Place potatoes and sweet potatoes on paper
  towels to drain.

Place potatoes in a bowl. Add onion, eggs,
  salt, pepper, and matzo meal, and stir
  until blended.

Heat oil in a large frying pan until very hot.

Very carefully drop a tablespoonful of potato
  batter into the pan. (Watch out for
  spattering oil.)

Fry batter until golden brown on both sides.

Serve with chunky applesauce or sour
  cream.

Serves four people.

Hanukkah Treats

Many Jewish people eat sweet treats during Hanukkah. In Eastern Europe, Jewish people might eat latkes with applesauce. In Israel and other countries in the Middle East, a popular Hanukkah food is a fried doughnut that is covered with powdered sugar. Jewish people in Spain eat a ball of fried dough that is dipped in honey. Like latkes, fried pastries remind Jewish people of the oil that lasted for eight days. They also taste delicious!

In the United States, Jewish families follow their own Hanukkah **traditions**. They often eat the foods that their **ancestors** ate. If their relatives came to America from the Middle East, they might make fried doughnuts at Hanukkah. If their relatives lived in Eastern Europe, then they probably eat latkes with applesauce.

16

Fresh Chunky Applesauce

You will need:

8 medium tart apples (Granny Smith or Pippin)

1 tablespoon (15 ml) water

¼ cup (59 ml) sugar

½ teaspoon (2.5 ml) ground cinnamon

¼ teaspoon (1.2 ml) ground cloves

2 tablespoons (30 ml) butter

How to do it:

Peel apples and remove cores. Place apples in a large saucepan.

Add sugar, cinnamon, cloves, and 1 tablespoon (15 ml) of water to the apples.

Cover pan. Heat on stove until ingredients boil.

Turn down heat, and simmer the apples for 15 minutes.

Check for tenderness by piercing with a fork.

If not tender, simmer for another 5 minutes.

Remove pan from heat and add remaining butter.

Mash with a potato masher or a wooden spoon.

Leave the apples somewhat chunky.

Serve hot or warm with latkes or as dessert with cookies.

Serves four people.

Cheese
at Hanukkah

Cheese is a food that many Jewish people enjoy during Hanukkah. This is because of the Bible story of Judith. Judith lived in the Jewish town of Bethulia, which was attacked by the Syrians. One evening, Judith visited the general of the Syrian army and fed him a dinner with a lot of cheese in it. The cheese made the general very thirsty, so he drank a lot of wine. The wine made him go to sleep, and while he was sleeping, Judith cut off his head. When they found their murdered general the next morning, the scared Syrian soldiers ran away. In this way, Judith saved her town from being attacked by the Syrians. Today, Jews eat cheese during Hanukkah to remember the story of Judith.

Baked Cheese Sticks

You will need:

8 ounces (227 grams)
    firm cheese
    (Cheddar or Swiss)
2 eggs
½ cup (119 ml) dry
    bread crumbs

How to do it:

Have an adult turn on the broiler of an oven.

Cut cheese into strips the same size as frozen fish sticks.

Crack the eggs over a large plate and beat well.

Spread bread crumbs on another plate.

Dip cheese sticks into egg mixture, one at a time.

Then, dip them into the bread crumbs. Shake off extra crumbs.

Place breaded cheese sticks onto a lightly oiled baking sheet.

Place baking sheet onto broiler rack. (Watch closely, because cheese sticks can burn quickly.) Remove pan once to turn sticks over.

Remove when crumbs turn nicely brown.

Serves four people.

Hanukkah Around the World

All around the world, Jewish people celebrate the eight days of Hanukkah. In Israel, Hanukkah is a national holiday. The schools there are closed for eight days, and everyone enjoys the celebration. In Morocco, Jewish families cook a different kind of food in oil each night.

Jewish people from Spain have a special party on the sixth night of Hanukkah, the night of the new moon. The dinner for this celebration probably includes cous-cous, which is a ricelike dish with lamb, onion, honey, raisins, and honey. In Turkey, children take plates of delicious sweet pastries to other families to give as gifts. In the United States, children often receive gifts each evening during Hanukkah.

Star of David Cookies

You will need:

½ cup (119 ml) cup butter

1 cup (237 ml) brown sugar

2 eggs

2 ¼ cups (533 ml) flour

2 teaspoons (10 ml) baking powder

1 teaspoon (5 ml) vanilla

Frosting in a tube (supermarket baking section)

How to do it:

Have an adult help you to preheat an oven to 350 degrees Fahrenheit (177 degrees C).

In a bowl, mix butter and brown sugar until light and creamy.

Add eggs, flour, baking powder, and vanilla. Mix until well blended.

Roll dough on a floured board or waxed paper.

Use a Star of David cookie cutter to cut out cookies.

Place cookies on a buttered cookie sheet.

Bake for 20 minutes until light brown.

When the cookies have cooled, outline the cookies with blue frosting. (Blue is a national color of Israel.)

Hanukkah Is Celebration

Although Hanukkah honors the bravery of the Jews in their battle with the Syrian armies, it is not a holiday that celebrates war. Hanukkah celebrates the light that came after the darkness of war. Hanukkah is a joyful holiday full of parties, feasting, gifts, singing, and games.

Jewish children play a game called dreidel during Hanukkah. A dreidel is a spinning top. Hebrew letters on the four sides of the dreidel stand for the sentence "A great miracle happened here." Dreidel is a fun way to remember the miracle that Hanukkah celebrates. Eating latkes and other good food is another fun way to celebrate this wonderful holiday.

Glossary

ancestors (AN-ses-turz) Relatives who lived long ago.

cycles (SY-kulz) Series of events that occur again and again.

defend (dih-FEND) To protect from attack or harm.

Hebrew (HEE-broo) Language spoken by ancient Jewish people and by Jews in Israel today.

Judaism (JOO-dee-ih-zum) The religion followed by Jews, based on teachings in the Old Testament of the Bible.

miracle (MEER-uh-kul) A wonderful event that is said to have been done by God.

new moon (NOO MOON) When the moon is shown as a thin crescent. Also, the first day of the month in the Jewish lunar calendar.

symbolize (SIM-buh-lyz) To stand for something important.

traditions (tra-DIH-shunz) Ways of doing things that are passed down through the years.

worship (WUR-ship) To pay great honor and respect to someone or something.

23

Index

Web Sites

To find out more about the celebration of Hanukkah, check out these Web sites:

www.ohr.org.il/special/chanukah/laws.htm

www.us-israel.org/jsource/Judaism/holiday7.html

24